STOWAWAYS

STOWAWAYS

Ariel Gordon

To Joan —
So very nice to meet you & to hear your work...

Copyright © 2014 Ariel Gordon
All rights reserved

Palimpsest Press
1171 Eastlawn Ave.
Windsor, Ontario. N8S 3J1
www.palimpsestpress.ca

Book and cover design by Dawn Kresan. Typeset in Onyx and Adobe Garamond Pro, and printed offset on Rolland Zephyr Laid at Coach House Printing in Ontario, Canada. Edited by Jim Johnstone.

Palimpsest Press would like to thank the Canada Council for the Arts, and the Ontario Arts Council for their support of our publishing program. We also acknowledge the assistance of the Government of Ontario through the Ontario Book Publishing Tax Credit.

Library and Archives Canada Cataloguing in Publication

Gordon, Ariel, 1973–, author
    Stowaways / Ariel Gordon.

Poems.
ISBN 978-1-926794-18-1 (pbk.)

    I. TITLE.

PS8613.O725S76 2014   C811'.6   C2014-900894-5

CONTENTS

1.

Highbeam   9
Bicker   10
Primipara   12
Belly   13
Lures   14
Wingless Females   15
Elbows   17
Thump   18
Headbutt   20
Stowaways   21
Blown   22
Sidewalk   23
Litter   24
Windfirm   25
Heart Attack   26
Picked Out   27
Pear Suite   29
Neck   31

2.

Little White Lie   35
Mother Goose   37
Pond Scum   38
Herd Instinct   39
Little Pig   41
Canis soupus   42

3.

How to Make a Collage   47
How to Treat Boils   49
How to Rip a Phonebook in Half   51
How to Keep a Relationship Fresh   53
How to Learn Morse Code   55
How to be a Prince Among Men   56
How to Survive in the Woods   58
How to Water Your Lawn Effectively   59
How to Prepare for Flooding   60
How to Sew a Button   62
How to be Angry in Public   64
How to Catch a Wild Rabbit   67
How to See Deer   69
How to Treat Leprosy   70
How to Pack Without Overpacking   71
How to Write a Poem   72

4.

How to Soften Facial Scars   75
Summer Weight   77
How to Tell if Someone is Dead   78
Song Of   80
Apparent Magnitude: the Finlay 15P   81
How to Survive a Plane Crash   87

NOTES   91
ACKNOWLEDGEMENTS   93
AUTHOR BIOGRAPHY   95

1.

"What do I say when someone calls me to say, 'There's a raccoon in my yard! Come trap it!' ?"

"Congratulations! You just saw wildlife!"

—Brian Joynt, Regional Wildlife Manager,
    Manitoba Conservation and Water Stewardship

Highbeam

Regurgitated rodent on the back steps. Sunken,
disheveled, it is the bog man
of field mice: murdered & concealed
in a body of water. I know this
is nothing. A dozen sneakered feet have washed up
along the Pacific the past five years.
Pleasure craft picked clean? Dumped cargo?
Bodies slowly coming apart,
salt-cured toes
acquiring a permanent prune.
Every scrap? Cats that arch their backs
deliciously when you're still
twenty feet away, highbeams eyes scanning
the sidewalk. My father, his headdress
of window-smashed birds & squirrels
softened in the soffit & fascia, his face going grey
under his tennis tan. Not knowing the difference
between soffit & fascia, between rescue
& medium-rare, the children
watching. Do you buy a gravestone for a Swoosh™
full of joints & bones? Do you shoebox spit-up mouse
or nestle it among the week's scraps
& hope no one notices?

Bicker

In the neighbour's yard, a pair of slim conifers.
Whose resident merlins shriek,

bickering from streetlight to elm canopy
& back all through the summer

until the adolescent broke his wing, dragging
it through the grass,

past the white housecat
& all its off-white teeth, past the man

from two doors down
who said, *Leave it, it's fine.* We packed

the merlin in Tupperware™, the big blue bin
that keeps basement floodwater

from our copies of *National Geographic*,
kept our eyes off him all night

before driving birdy to the wildlife rehab centre
in the morning. Wanting to say goodbye.

But to what? To the *thud*
as he misjudged his perch? To the oomph

of the nesting pair, his parents,
who abandoned their borrowed nest

the next summer? Or to the missed opportunity
of the neighbourhood cats? (Feathers

& entrails everywhere: my yard, your yard,
the middle of the sidewalk.)

Tonight, there is only the *purr*
of lawnmowers

as I wash his agonized turds
off the towel that lined the bottom

of the bin.

Merlins: *ki-ki-kee*

Primipara

> "A woman who is pregnant for the first time or who has borne just one child."
> —*Webster's New World Dictionary*

If I had had twins, I would have eaten one.

If I had had twins, I would have cracked
a beatific smile. *Thanks,*
but no. And primly given it/them back.

If I had had twins, I would have tucked
them under my arms like footballs or small perfect
hand-grenades aimed at my breasts: *fuck.*

If I had had twins, I would have kept mum.

Belly

Chunk of blubber. Obtained at great gory cost, it somehow
makes light. Enough to fill the evenings, all of us bent
over our work.

Inner tube. A gorgeous buoyancy.

Curbside snow bank: by-product of scraped streets,
instant Everest. Irresistible to small children.

Bubbling wallpaper over softening plaster and lathe.
(The house folds but doesn't do windows.)

Clutch purse containing a coil of worry beads.

Starving animal. First, you were indigestion and then,
a ten-course meal.

Quinzee. You tunneled out, your shoulder blade
a shovel, your jabbing elbow
a pick. It collapsed behind you. A collapsed
quinzee is just a shrinking pile
of snow.

Stranded whale, its blowhole sighing
at intervals.

Pillow where you left
the impression of your face.

Lures

We found teeth on the sand at Victoria Beach
& a bleached skull whose beak rested
comfortably on my daughter's wrist. Now I sit on the deck
of this borrowed cabin while birds strip-mine
front yards, the flock moving methodically
from one lawn to the next. Black birds, pecking at parcels
of grass, freshly mown. They could be grackles,
from a page of the bird book I haven't yet turned.
The leaves—dusty, full of holes—are clearly contemplating it.
Hard to imagine now spring's precarious eggs, that first fling
into mid-air. *Here? There?* My daughter's chirp plain
half-a-block away, her fingers buried
in her dad's dry palm. (Her fingers lures
& both of us hungry.) The flock lifts
over the twilight screams of half-grown kids on bikes,
tires on gravel as they screech angrily,
exultantly to the second street-light & back: their line
in the sand. Our pediatrician measures my daughter's head
religiously but we haven't yet figured out
her boundaries.

Grackles: *readle-eak*

Wingless Females

I wanted a single flower
in a vase
for the party.

I sent my daughter to cut
the first peony from the volunteer
on our gravel driveway:

she hesitated
wanting to use the big scissors
but not sure where to cut

or how to insinuate herself
into the peony's wet stalks,
its raised fists

swollen with small red ants.
She looked at me,
her face a crumpled tissue.

Here. Look. I said.
I took the kitchen shears
from her small hand.

Dew on my legs, dirty car
still warm at my back,
I reached down into the heart

of the plant
& cut the stalk long,
stripping away extra leaves

with the practiced impatience
of a smoker stripping plastic
from a fresh pack:

the bathroom
still needed cleaning
inside.

Before going back in
I shook off the dew
& a small brown spider.

Later, one of my sisters killed
three ants—
wingless sterile females

called workers—
on the dinner table
& when the party was finished

I saw two ants floating
in the vase
& the peony was as shabby

as the jumbled mass
of factory-made valentines
I'd unearthed that morning

from a drawer,
my daughter's name
everywhere.

Elbows

Sloppy kisses.

Clanging pipes, a smear
of solder on the threads.

Concealed weapons: Hatpins?
Switchblades?

Scraps of crispy skin, the carcass laid bare.

Swollen rivers jumping
their banks, looking
for the path of least resistance.

Brick shithouses.

Thump

Geese ankle-deep in slush,
necks like slow songs & beer-slippery hands
outstretched in rough bars,
grip & batter each other
beneath trees:

Thump.

Further in, fallen wasps' nests, all sweet
pulp & chitin, get caught up in sudden breezes
& roll to the tree-line
where moss melts snow.

Further in, pellets scatter
amidst bleached grasses in the rounded
spaces between trees, a recollection of warmth
where deer knelt.

At the edge of the clearing, stumps
& the charred stillness
where the single-engine plane
touched down:

Thump.

Nearby, boys in shirtsleeves turn
backs on spring's riffling fingers
& grit whirlwinds,
flash knobby spines under fabric pulled tight,
fabric snatched away.

Under the trees, ragged mushrooms
& splayed ribs emerge from ice as trains clatter by
& fat horses delicately cross tracks, hooves
striking steel:

Thump.

Geese: *hisssssssssss*

Headbutt

In the car dealership waiting room, all ammonia & rubber & non-fat dairy creamer, sits a fish tank the width of a mid-size sedan. An angelfish watches me wait for my car, retreating behind the curtain of bubbles from a knocked-over pagoda when I look at her too directly. I am charmed by her demure attentions & trailing fins the way the brassy medium on the wall-mounted TV charms her studio audience by dangling reassuring messages from the dead. Until the angelfish headbutts another fish who ventures over. The dead likely as incoherent as the rest of us.

Stowaways

On the way home, we squashed stowaway
mosquitoes against the windows & picked
burrs from our socks, dropping them onto the mats
& if there were any horseflies beating
against the windshield
where it narrowed
to the thinnest
slice of sky,
we ignored them.

I was glaring at the roof of the car
when I saw the wood tick
on your neck & when you lowered
the window & tossed it out, its legs skittered
against the dry ridges of skin
on your thumb. As we watched, the sky grew:
we could see all the things that floated
in it & the effort
it took
to remain aloft,
dragonflying & dying across the glass.

Blown

Bouquet of balloons in the back seat.
My daughter swats, adding fingerprints
to the latex covering drifting fists
of noble gas. In the rearview I get glimpses of road,
her heated cheeks, the cars nudging
the few feet between us
at the lights. I don't ever expect more
than glimpses. How we both got a mouthful
of crabapple pulp today when all she was after
was a single bloom. How she substituted dandelion
for daisy when the oldest charm
rattled through her head: *She loves me,
she loves me not.* And started shedding yellow.
Lately, she's relied on *I didn't mean to…*
Which means everything I own shredded,
everything I own fragile. Like a balloon
floating into the front seat, static
electricity
a kiss with teeth.

Sidewalk

Strip mall across from the old stadium. Mid-afternoon moon
of floodlights in the grey sky as on-foot Bomber fans
round corners, strain yellow lights.

Flight of abandoned umbrellas overhead. Hum of buses
& cars, hot dog cart smoking on the sidewalk. How distant
my daughter's fingers feel through mittens.

Across the street, the bundled-up crowd roars.
A swell of sound rolls across St. James Avenue, bounces
off Old Navy™ & across the parking lot:

over the bright sweater a shopper picked out
for her nephew and the deeply-discounted pants
her husband just couldn't pass up,

to the man behind the hot dog cart, greasy apron
yoked over his parka, transistor radio blaring:
Touchdown! And you know everyone's found themselves

on their feet, fists raised, praise pouring
out of mouths. And the score is migratory waterfowl
vs. rats with wings, imported football players

vs. domestic beer, sweet communion
vs. seasonal sales. At dinner, my daughter's socked foot
works the long muscle in my thigh

like she's flooring it. Like it all matters.

Geese: *honk*

Litter

> "Tired of seeing cigarette butts? Over one quarter of the litter you see on streets comes from cigarettes. See the plan to clean up our city."
> —CBC Manitoba Facebook newsfeed, August 20, 2010.

One quarter of the litter you see
on streets is lipstick-ed cigarette butts.

One third is mosquito & house fly
carcasses, which rustle
& snap when stepped on.

City workers build buzzing pyres
every few weeks. We disperse
after they're lit, satisfied.

One eighth is old-school Jets™ jerseys,
arms flung wide.

One quarter is pigeon
& pigeon parts, inclusive of the brown
beer glass & grit in their crops
but not the sharp raptors overhead.

Four-point-two per cent is grubby
dandelion bouquets.

Seeping milk.

Peregrine falcons: *kak-kak-kak*

Windfirm

On my way out of the house, my daughter asked to borrow my lip-gloss, then pressed a glittery O on the sleeve of my raincoat. My mother had had an immunization scar in the same spot. I used to touch it as often as I could. I would have licked it if she'd let me.

Badminton between two boulevard elms. One is windfirm, the other a widowmaker, dropping hundreds of pounds of pulp every time it storms. In the last of the sun, in the long grass, my daughter sprints after the plastic birdie: an imitation of an imitation of a bird in flight.

For a few weeks, I had a ladybird on the curtain near my bed & a small hot foot on my thigh. The aphid-eater hibernating or dead. My daughter asleep, again, in our bed. I had a six-spotted beetle on the yellow curtains my mother sewed for our first house. My daughter's slack cheeks, bright pink, as though sleeping warm was a great exertion. The day I wanted to make a poem out of them, I found the dusty ladybug on the floor next to a snarl of my hair.

Heart Attack

Wormy apple. Balled fist.

Fingers going white,
bloody marks on your palm—
suckerpunch.

Filet mignon on a plate,
spoiling.

Obstinate dud.
To be disposed of.
Red/blue wires crossed.

Bloody handful.

The house you grew up in,
on fire.

Rotten egg & the hand cupping it
& the arm pitching it.

Jerky knee
to the nuts.

Jack in the box
with a bent lid. Its jaunty tune.

Picked Out

The particulars of today's pick: a man
in safety glasses who's just been laid off,
coming into a pear tree
he must learn to prune back,

upper branches like outstretched arms. We find
him deep in the tree & are soon slashed
& leafy from its limbs.
The girl sprints

after pears that plummet
to the ground, swift judgment, avoiding
rigid legs of ladders, the slide
of rotten pears

on grass. The tree full of leaning ladders,
but that ladder is only for him:
He wouldn't trust it to hold anyone else
and he would hate … but we all want

the blushing flanks of pears high in the tree.
By any means. Knowing squirrels take
tiny indiscriminate bites.
Knowing our buckets are timely.

We pull down a hundred & thirty pounds,
a slack body of pears. We weigh them
in bins & boxes on a pink bathroom scale
on the sidewalk. The pears a flock

of greenish birds lined up at a feeder.
The pears as painful as new breasts.
The man brings out the pears
he picked last week

& they glow: *Pears, yeah.*
But a hundred pounds of pears
just for me?
I can't give them away

quickly enough. We nod, all of us understanding
the anxiety of rotting fruit,
the dotted line that divides my yard
from your yard.

And then he shows us
the picking tool he rigged up: a plastic bag
& a broom handle. And all I want for him
is hours contemplating the sky

through branches.
Days with his hands way over his head
&, every year, a yard full of strangers,
as efficient as locusts.

Pear Suite

The girl shouts from the bath: *I'm hungry.*
I sit on the lip & fit wedges of yellow
pear in her mouth.

Remembering how the green fruit gleamed
in my palm, how my feet fit
in the tree's sturdy crotch.

The girl reading on the front step.
In utero, in the bath, her elbow skimmed
the smooth skin of my belly. Last week, wracked

with fever, the girl fell asleep
in the tub, loose hands magnified
by the bath's prism. Her soft snores, her sharp chin

floating just above water level.
Thirty pounds of pears stored
on our screened-in porch.

I owe that man a crisp.

    *
People with fruit trees often speak
with false hilarity of leaving some for the squirrels.

For the birds.

It looks like riches in their arms,
they think, as the fruit is baled & boxed

& stowed in cars.
It looks like I gave it all away.

    *

The pears have aged without me,
slowly softening through the afternoons.
Sharp knife, the thick skin on the tip
of my thumb nicked

again. The pear-shaped hole in my face,
ringed with yellowed teeth,
mornings
& afternoons of small sips of tea.
All my grandmother's cups of weak milky tea

in one mug. How her skin thinned
to nothing.
My father a big watery pear.

    *

I cut up the last perfect pear, firm & cool,
& sent it in the girl's lunch.

It came back browned. I prized open
the Tupperware™

& gulped the soft bit down.

Neck

Shaded glen.

Illuminated manuscript,
all albumen, gold,
& ruddy light.

Network of tubing
attached to a heavily-medicated patient.

Safe haven, her wet
face set there.

Xylem & phloem clothed in bark.

Subway map.

Fretwork. Your fingers.
This thrumming chord.

2.

"For it is said to be the nature of women that they produce as offspring whatever they see or imagine at the height of their ardour as they conceive; animals, indeed, when they are mating, transmit inwardly the forms they see outwardly and, imbued with these images, take on their appearance as their own."
—Folio 23v, *Aberdeen Bestiary*

Little White Lie

After Raffi's Baby Beluga

I met him on a two-hour tour of Churchill's ice floes.

The belugas in my pod felt the click of shutters on us & in us as tourists leaned out over the water, their devices reassuring them: *This moment. Yes. You've got it.*

He was a tourist but he sat on the boat, his hands empty. His hands empty & his eyes drifting from snout to side. I was the smallest, the one always on the extreme edge of the pod. But I crept closer, the blue as water as his eyes…

Later, he told me his smartphone was in his pocket, battery drained.

Or he would have been all over me.

That night, confused by meltwater, I circled the harbour's plastic junk & beached myself when I saw him, thin & drunk & knee-deep in slush.

He'd wandered, windburnt, out of the bar, his adventure gear bright foolishness on the scree but when I rose from the surf, he clasped me so gratefully, his nipples small hard stones against my chest … I thought he recognized me.

On the way to his room, I adjusted the drape of my skin—dingy towel—around my shoulders & discovered what it was to shiver. He muttered & held me tight, as if I was a sperm whale and my skull made light enough for two.

Three years later, my skin—dirty laundry—was in the baby-bag. But he left it on the front porch, brought only his credit card to the hospital.

The labour was as long as that first night in the tangle of his arms, as slow as the tundra-train back to Winnipeg in the morning. I'd wanted to give birth in water, to wash the baby out, my skin—frayed rag—shaping her, but the big-city birthing center was delayed and badly over-budget.

So I bore down in a bed, my mouth full of ice chips. I bore down, his fingers rubbing my lower back, his palm measuring out my spine.

Mother Goose

I was always long-necked, thick through the waist & broody, but being with child cinched it.

Some women knit booties, spend months learning how to turn the heel. Others become morbidly interested in pastels. Me, I yanked out my hair, hank by hank, lining the crib with the long black stuff.

(By the time baby lifted her hand to me, all she'd find were licks of down…)

The crib was soft, the crib was soft, but skin-to-skin is best, they say & I was all ruddy, starving skin, feeding her at all hours, reduced to dining by the fridge's stark light those times she settled.

(She seemed to know when I'd had enough & would rouse, squawking arms out-thrust.)

My hair grew in but my weight dropped like a wet crow. Her father started bringing home crumpled take-out bags, subs half-eaten, or withered fruit out of season, strawberries wooden, the apples sharp; shoddy groceries to be sure, but what can you do when your baby is never further away than the tips of your outstretched fingers?

I tried to tell him: *What's good for the goose is good for the gander.*

But he learned early the nine-to-five was salvation after the dim all-day-all-night of our love nest. And if by some trick of the light he got lonely, all he had to do was stand at Portage/Main & listen to the sirens.

Pond Scum

After the Brothers Grimm's The Frog Prince

He was a yodeling country western singer from Quebec.

I was Queen of the St. Malo Frog Follies & our first time was in a motel hot tub, his green eyes glinting with light reflected from my tiara.

I was Anglo through & through … but I liked his accent.

My mother told me frogs were slippery, charmers that never settled anywhere long, but I thought. *I'm his special princess.* I thought. *Having children will change him.*

Nine months later, my young are squirming thoughts in my mouth & he's still half-frog, half cad.

There was the Queen Mermaid in Flin Flon. A Butter Princess in Minnesota … he even hooked up with a Miss Teen Canada on a pit stop in Oshawa.

I used to put Vaseline™ on my teeth when I competed. I flossed & whitened religiously. I could taste the waves of applause as they rolled over me.

But now I keep my mouth shut so I don't blurt out my babies.

And my smile is a *caulisse* heartbreaker.

Herd Instinct

In late spring, the ponds at Fort Whyte are full of broken broomhandles & sodden wrapping-paper tubes & none of us believe in growth or re-growth or even babies that get up hours after birth.

But out in the pasture, afterbirth cures like sausage between my sister-wife's legs as her calf hobbles over ruts & wallows.

When the calf is eight months old, its headbutts to my sister-wife's udder will almost unseat her; she will be almost as bruised as when she presented herself to the prairie, backside open & raw, the male a dark cloud nearby.

In late spring, the ponds at Fort Whyte fill with lusty frog-song & shorebirds that shriek sleek counterpoint & the sound washes over me as though through skin.

Footsore, bored, my daughter spins so she can fall & she spins so she can see me again & again & she spins to spin & fall.

Three years ago, the male emerged from aspen woods, his thick coat thrown open, his bare skin steaming…

Today, the pond offers marbled sheets of algae & waterweed, silence & din & I want to stay at the edge of the pasture. I want to lean into his deep shadow.

Her stepdad catches my eye & begins to carry my daughter away but she believes in me even through a screen of willow, its branches buckshot with galls: *Mum-mum! Mum-mum!*

Out in the pasture, my sister-wife is delivered from the humpbacked sway of her pregnant sisters & stands apart.

Mum-mum!

Out in the pasture, the calf, sensitive to fillips of movement, jumps as the tractor works the other half of their range ... as I give up & cart my daughter off.

Little Pig

After Maurice Sendak's Where the Wild Things Are

I am a bricky pig. I always thought myself safe, my four walls, fire in my Whyte Ridge hearth but maybe I saw a wolf on the hill one night & maybe I wanted to be a wolf & maybe I met the wolf through my lit window, her out in the dark in her moonlit rooms, blood on her muzzle, maybe.

So I birthed a wolf, squealing.

Wolves den, don't they? Burrow under rocks, keep young buried as though in graves, their eyes shining in sudden painful light as they tumble like laundry, biting & kissing all at once.

My boy was born pink & squirming, suckling noisily. My husband grunted with satisfaction as he went to work, his son keening. *Colic*, they said. But I went to work too, stopping up the spill of sunlight across our rooms, hanging drapes & blinds & taping sheets of foil across every edge, but still: sun!

When we found a wolf costume at a jumble sale it helped. He was no longer a naked thing who must be dressed neatly & then also slathered in Banana Boat™ Kids SPF 50. Every pink inch of him was covered.

And so, in our dim rooms, he went as a wolf.

Until I found him standing over the still-warm body of my husband's fat little Highland Terrier. Bloody fork in hand, the cuffs of his ragged costume red. I stripped him. I stripped him down, shrouded it in black plastic & hurtled it into the auto-bin. With the body.

My husband squealed when I said the pup had somehow. gotten. out.

Canis soupus

The first clue was how he *yipped* instead of laughing. How the sound bounced off the living room wall. And came back at us.

He was wonky in the way that teenage boys are, rough-boned, stinky.

He slunk around the house, almost never looking us in the eye. He almost never said thank you, though we kept the fridge full and his iTunes™ account topped up.

We thought it was pot. Or jerking off.

We lingered at his bedroom door for tell-tale odours. For *oh-oh-Oh-OH!*

We could have offered him the good stuff. Or made wink-wink comments about hairy palms. But we tried to leave him be.

Until he started wandering around St. Vital at night, shirtless. Until I watched him watching the neighbour through her living room window, his exposed skin glowing.

His nipples were a shock. It had been years since I'd seen that much of him. And he was so very naked…

So, standing in the dark kitchen, I tracked him. Silverware gleaming in its drawer. A chicken defrosting on the counter, its legs securely trussed.

I took prenatal vitamins. I opted for a natural birth. But even so, I knew there were risks: he could have arrived with a clubfoot or a heart murmur.

But I was unprepared when I saw how his coyote's head was torqued backwards on his shoulders, that night in our yard.

I heard him struggle to howl, his windpipe obstructed. I heard him trying to breech-birth himself, out in the dark.

And that's how I found myself, howling sympathetically by the fridge's harsh light.

Come in, I tried to tell him. *I'll feed you.*

3.

"Subjects for sensitive poems: autumn, death, pain, trees, the cosmos, critics, beauty, clouds, suicide, dreaming, leaves, yourself, loneliness, futility, blight, depression, decay, loss, entropy, love, flowers, branches, tree stumps."
    —From *How to be a Sensitive Poet* by Matt Groenig

How to Make a Collage

Toilet paper taken from the bottom of a shoe while in company.

My grandfather wrote us letters from South Africa on blue airmail stationary that had to be slit open. The eyelid-thin paper was shaped by the marks from his pen, by the pressure of his hands on the paper, holding it all still. As a teenager, I liked to imagine him on a balcony overlooking the pool, bathed in cool blue light & the faintest chlorine pong. I liked to imagine avocados hanging like breasts over him. I liked to imagine him sweating.

How a fire always turns & lays a tail of smoke over your tearing eyes.

Clumped tissues
a mouthful of flesh pinched
from my grandmother's
radiation-singed inner arm.

A five-dollar bill with MOVE OUT written across Sir Wilfred Laurier's pursed lips.

In the spring, during break-up, we opened our nighttime windows & laid in bed listening to the river's thousand tinkling chandeliers, its thousand jaws crushing cubes. In the dark, uprooted trees & unmoored docks & lawn chairs on giant slabs of ice…

Tiny baby teeth & pitted wisdoms in a used greeting-card envelope.

My belly is bubbling wallpaper over softening plaster & lathe. This refrain is a floating rib, attached to the body using the traditional methods: clippings from the *Winnipeg Free Press*, Safeway™ bags, photographs & foil.

How to Treat Boils

"Tip #1: Apply a slice of a raw potato to the affected area. Raw cabbage leaf is also very good for reducing inflammation and promoting healing."
—"How to Treat Boils," *wikiHow*

The body shows the work of viruses & bacteria as if it was a canvas, an entire gallery's worth of canvases: boils, impetigo, prickly heat rash, rosacea, scarlet fever, swimmer's itch, thrush.

The body painted, pinked by ointments. The body lowered inch-by-fevered-inch into oatmeal baths, bloodstream flush with antihistamines & steroids.

Tell me, do you prefer annato in a vial or the hemoglobin in your veins? Yellow fever or FD&C Yellow NO. 5™?

Skin is a thin shield.

*

Good-time god of fields, groves & wooded glens, Pan was half-man, half-goat. He'd eat anything. Grumpy goddess of parking lots, golf courses & managed green spaces, I'm half-woman, half-gout. I gulp water like wine & gnaw seeping handfuls of woody berries.

    *
Sperm swarm an enormous, indifferent egg.

A full club: badly-lit bodies besiege the bar, bills bristling from outstretched hands.

Buckshot launches at a doe's plump hindquarters, her head buried in the brush, her mouth working.

    *
When treating mumps, custom decrees wrapping the face, jaw & jowls with linseed poultices. If cloth bandages are unavailable, strips torn from your petticoats or the drapes (or even petticoats made from drapes) make for acceptable substitutes. (Likewise, hot toddies & rum punches can be spontaneously swapped for freshly squeezed milk & thin broth.) Tie the poultices firmly. Your knots should resemble meaty chestnuts, roasting on a hearth.

How to Rip a Phonebook in Half

You've heard of cooking the books?

An apple pie in the oven is a realtor's trick. But bake a phonebook for twenty minutes and you're the man—a reeking mix of ink & commerce & industry.

The paper might be brittle but the applause won't be…

Postcards
Pamphlets
Term papers
Parliamentary reports
Thinly-plotted paperbacks

Make three hundred paper airplanes. You will be so practiced at your craft that you could put out the eye of the pretty new math teacher. If you wanted to.

One heaping scoop of protein powder after another.
A personal gym paid off in installments.
A tendency towards Spandex™.

There is no such thing as 'a phonebook.' You live in a particular place.

Feats of strength favour those living in supervillages, in RMs and along rural routes. Attempting the NYC phonebook is like filling in the NYT crossword in pen.

You can empty out your local phonebook by converting everyone to cell phones. Slogans are key:

You might as well have a landmine in your yard as a landline in your living room!

Cell phones are to thinking people as pacemakers are people riddled with heart disease! Saviours!

Eat a five-pound hamburger because you're, like, really hungry. Enter a twenty-four hour dance marathon even if you have to resort to jazz hands. Shave every square inch of your body ... just to see what it feels like.

Now. Take a hold of the book and STRAIN.

How to Keep a Relationship Fresh

> "Tip #4: Try new things in the bedroom and out! For instance, barring health issues such as rheumatoid arthritis or gout, men should be able to bring female partners to orgasm with their big toe while sitting across from them at a table."
> —"How to Keep a Relationship Fresh," *wikiHow*

I try to imagine your toe working
its way out of its tired boot
while we wait
for crispy ginger beef, clacking
our battered plastic chopsticks like beaks:
all the soft creases between thumb
& forefinger they have laid in, all the grateful lips
& teeth & tongues
they have been raised to.

I try to conceive
of your callused toe lifting
from its dusty sandal some Saturday morning:
it has all somehow been many years
of the same Saturday, both of us looking for
& finding pleasure
at the bottom of diner mugs,
our daughter coloring at your elbow,
hoping her pancakes will be poured out with ears,
that the cook at the grill has looked out
& seen her bowed head.

Your linty toe sliding
across the lino at your parents',
your sock's thin protection left under your chair
as I pass the roast & the potatoes,
the everyday china seasoned
by your resemblance
to your uncle, our daughter's resemblance
to your mother. The long exhale of these years?
Peppery kisses on my forehead
as you go by but also: small piles
of toenail clippings
forgotten on the bedside table.

How to Learn Morse Code

"Tip #4: To indicate that you have made a mistake while broadcasting the previous word, transmit eight dots. This will tell the receiver of your message to cross out the last word transmitted before the signal."
—"How to Learn Morse Code," *wikiHow*

For dots, put peppercorns on your tongue. Swallow. Repeat. Sprawl on the grassy berm just behind the mall. Listen: trucks-in-reverse are to loading docks as tagged whales are to breeding grounds. Sounding frequently. *Um.* When the zombie apocalypse comes, your tippity-tap skills will be on par with those who can kill remorselessly........ pitilessly. Oily fingerprints on a door. Dried raindrops on a window. Soft fingertips on your inner arm. Never mind the mother-of-invention. What you need is the aggressive step-father: loads of free time & a touch of OCD. For dashes, put peppercorns between your molars. Grind them down. In a moment of crisis: your thrumming heart in your chest & your buzzing phone in your breast pocket.

How to be a Prince Among Men

After Nicolo Machiavelli's The Prince

When out hunting, be excessively friendly to doddery old women standing RIGHT in the MIDDLE of the ROAD. Similarly, refrain from goring white does with *yeux affronte*.

Remember, be PLEASANT to the peasants!

If you come across a catatonic girl in a castle or glass coffin in the woods, don't assume a kiss is the only answer. Try jostling her first, unless, that is, you WANT to get bethrothed—they don't put spells on chambermaids!

N.B. If you MUST kiss her, under no circumstances should both feet EVER leave the turf.

For those rulers new to the princely arts, PLEASE, take a moment to think on your coat of arms. You'll be looking at that haddock *hauriant* or busty griffin for the REST of your life.

The WORST thing you can do is put away a sword bloody.

When you slay a monster—or have a rival assassinated—DO NOT rush in & claim all the loot. Tend to wounds. The treasure will still be there after you've thanked your team for their efforts.

Crown princes, remember your neck-strengthening exercizes. NO ONE wants to see a king with flaccid neck muscles! Just tense your nape & shoulders for ten seconds, then relax for another ten. Repeat three times, twice a day & you're well on your way to holding your head—and crown—high!

Here's an action item for all you crusaders out there: if you & three footmen can't carry it, you SHOULDN'T pack it.

If you're asked to secure the bloodline by marrying the cousin who nosebleeds when you look at her, don't fret. A few minutes of work & you'll be back to your butterfly collection.

How to Survive in the Woods

In the woods, the man who took off
his pants to spook fat dog walkers
& ancient slow birders
can't get it up. Nearby, the foreleg of a deer in a tree.

The first joint cleaned to the bone.
The furred knee hung over
a knot is a drunk uncle leaning close to say,
Nice gams! Knowing the poacher's stiff

with satisfaction at the gesture. And the woods are lousy
with teenagers, fingering guns of compressed air
& held breaths, so the first time
the woods come out & ask *Who are you?*

its voice breaks. You can marshal yourself against
the bloody leer of unleashed dogs,
the gnashed throats of mallards, but you can't plan
for the glimpse

between trees
of childhood in the clearing,
the slide of city shoes on the shield's chipped teeth,
how the word *wild* has begun to beg,

as a half-starved
bear begs: defeated, but with one eye
on the toddlers
& lap dogs.

How to Water Your Lawn Effectively

Drink so much water that you run clear & mark your territory, you dribbling homeowner you. Being neither a cooper nor a carpenter, invest in (the sour emptiness of) whiskey barrels. Invest in eaves, mulch plugs, ladders with slippery rungs—no ladder!—the intersect of lightning & elm canopy. Your neighbour's hose, 4 a.m. (Dreams of running water, of loss.) Mouth to bronze spout, you know: this is what happens when the nail in your vein is loosened. This is the taste of a mouthful of change. Rip out grass like carpet, like end-roll hastily bought & rejected by the next tenant who 'has an eye for these things.' Tramp dirt, raising peaty clouds & lining your mouth with sod. Avoid relationships with classical scholars prone to grand gestures or at least get one on a low-sodium diet. Ask a farmer if you can pick rocks (his fields overturned, rocks come to the surface as teeth come through gums). Don't think about drunks, vitrines & convenient projectiles. Train moss onto your rocks the way you train pets onto paper. Turn on the sprinkler. Lie on the lawn, aching & chill. When your hair is plastered among blades, your fingers twined with half-drowned worms, turn off the damn water.

How to Prepare for Flooding

The news says: *Flood! Recession! Flood!*
But you have to drive across the city to see the surge
& your ugly old basement is dry
& your guts mutter: *Spring!*
The same way your guts sometimes say
…*storm* at three a.m., windows rattling with wind & rain
& elm branches as your love sleeps
through, his rattling nostrils
almost drowned out.

And the river? It's high enough that the tidy back yards
of the houses by the river are filled with ice
& the elms in the tidy back yards
of the houses by the river are bracketed by ice.
And you can see how one tree has been uprooted by ice,
how it will slowly
tip into the river once the days
heat up again. But there are no sandbag dikes
& no homeowners passing antiques out
of upper windows & maybe their basements burp
and slosh but maybe not, so you go home.

Once parked, you see the enormous clump of slush
& ice & sand where weather systems have gathered
behind the wheels of your car. You kick it
& a hunk drops, as satisfying as a tooth
finally giving way, as a gout
of blood where a tooth was
or a baby dropping
after a fall & a winter & a wet spring
carrying it.

If you leave the hunk there, you will have to back
the car over it blind
& slushy, so you kick it over
to the garage door & out into the alley
but not far enough: every time you leave
the house it crunches under your tires, turning back
into snow, into silty water & grit
& as you drive under expensive shoes twirling
from overhead wires, under strange eyes
of men leaning from windows
of ugly old apartment blocks
you finally get it: *Flood. Recession.
Flood.*

How to Sew a Button

Wear the shirt, touching yourself where the hole is several times an hour, absently, deliberately.

Ask women of a certain age for safety pins, admiring the outstretched feet / slightly hunched backs as they rake the bottom of their bags.

Listen solemnly as they exclaim:

> *So many pens!*

Make them pin it on.

*

Wipe the top of your dresser with the shirt, balled up but warm from your skin, your tired armpits.

The outline of your fingers in dust on the shirt.

The frayed thread.

*

Decamp to a nice hotel. (Drunk, intimidated by the clean room, the dirty mattress.)

Open the travel kit on the bed like it was a tray of sterilized instruments stolen from a hospital & you were about to take a kidney from an immigrant.

*

Stab yourself a few times with the needle, artfully tangle the thread, bleed.

Take the mess to a co-worker.

Recoil from her sharp eyes.

*

Set up your tripod. Sew the shirt while still wearing it. Post the video to YouTube™.

*

Visit co-habitating friends wearing the shirt & a charmingly wistful expression. Hold your stomach in while your shirt is being mended & you stand barechested in the kitchen, reading the grocery list posted on the fridge.

> *eggs*
> *milk*
> *bananas*
> *foil*

The woman leaning over your shirt…

*

Rip the shirt into thin strips. Eat the shirt, strip by strip. Save the loose button for last.

How to be Angry in Public

Sticks are good & are usually just lying around. Only those completely comfortable with public displays of anger (or PDA) should try to improvise weapons from parking signs, ice scrapers & fence posts. Once a weapon has been obtained, whip it around your head until you hear a whistling noise. Beat a boulevard tree until you feel faintly ashamed.

Nobody owns the trees.

*

Make your eyes as flying daggers.

Or incendiary lasers.

Walk away really REALLY fast, hair whipping around your face.

*

Glass—frosted, silvered, clear—is particularly good. Storm windows can be picked up cheaply at garage & estate sales for just this purpose. Keep them in your garage or weedy back yard until you are ready. Mirrors have an intriguing psychological component but they also raise the spectre of bad luck. And superstition will just compete with the pureness of your anger.

Note #1: Closed-toe footwear and/or industrial work gloves are preferable for this exercise.

Note #2: In case of emergency, frozen-over puddles can also be smashed.

*

Jump up & down, hands clenched at your sides.

It isn't called 'hopping mad' for NOTHING.

If this doesn't help, fall down. A pile of leaves is good.

The cold/hard ground works too.

*

Shout *Hey* several times at the object of your anger while she walks away. For variation, try *Hey you!* & *Where are you going?* & even *Come back here, you!* Essential to this display of anger is the pace: back & forth two or three steps is good. Look twitchy—cheeks flushed, whites of eyes showing—as though you might lope after her at any moment. But stay where you are. Mutter *What are YOU looking at?* when people get within a three-foot radius.

*

Here's an anger role-play to get you in the mood:

Woman A: *Fuck you!*
Woman B: *No, fuck you!*
Woman A: *FUCK YOU, you Fuck!*
Woman B: *Arrrrrrgh! Blargh!*

For use when women are on opposite sides of busy roads or being successfully restrained by spouses or members of one's book club.

*

Mid-summer, neighbours & relatives will often gift you with surplus produce. Alternatively, you can grow what's called an 'anger garden.' Cabbages, pumpkins & watermelons have the same density as the human head, but for instant anger gratification, find a nice ripe tomato.

Squeeze & then squeeze tighter.

How to Catch a Wild Rabbit

We chased a rabbit through the creeping charlie
to the swing set's blue candy cane struts.
Mint rose from the pulped leaves between our toes
as the repellent on our legs lifted paint.

We passed Mum's big yellow mixing bowl between us
as we scuttled in dirty circles, the hill down to the river
a flounced hip, turning. The rabbit slow, unworried
& always out of reach.

We got ten minutes of telescoping ears & sidelong eyes
before the neighbour's cat snatched his neck
as if it was a purse left behind & reclaimed,
the warm full belly her wallet, her vital statistics.

The ginger cat, her mouth bristling, full,
the pinioned rabbit, staring.

We yelled as parents yell at seeing a child teeter
towards a blazing oven: *Sound! Gesture!* The cat, fat & full
& angry, dropped the body on the grass & left,
fur on her tongue. The rabbit lay there

before winching himself up & hobbling off,
neck pierced. I didn't have to imagine the sunset fox
patrolling the riverbank's beached elms
& shopping carts later, rabbit up its nose.

We set the bowl on the sun-lit counter & slunk away
from the chicken in the sink, the baby sister in the next room
snuffling at the breast, her hand shaking in abject pleasure,
in dumb bunny greeting.

But I could somehow imagine her lying
in the bowl, the light illuminating
the yellow plastic, picking out every blood vessel
in her floppy neck & her lying there, calm.

How to See Deer

Having spotted the tawny deer
in the managed forest of aspen clones,
we take three steps: *boots
on snow. Boots on snow.*

*Boots on snow.
Birdsong.* Rising out of re-introduced grasses
gone blonde in the sun, the doe is all weary ear
& ear & eye as we hop-step
another three strides: *boots on snow.
Boots on snow.*

Boots on snow. Birdsong. Our little herd
is ten feet off when she turns
& walks away, thick hips
& bow legs flashing
between trunks: *hooves on snow.
Hooves on snow.*

Hooves on snow. Twenty feet off,
the doe kicks at the ground, settles heavily
& disappears in the brush,
having decided we don't exist:

Birdsong.

Chickadees: *fee-bee*
Redpolls: *dreeee*

How to Treat Leprosy

When I am run down, I get cankers the size of overwintering ladybugs.

My favourite thing, mid-infection? To make people palpate the tender lymph nodes under my chin. Ow. OW! (*See?*)

Lyme Disease vectors include white-footed field mice, deer, raccoons, opossums, skunks, weasels, foxes, shrews, moles, chipmunks, squirrels & horses.

I once had a pebbly rash that almost completely enveloped my back & stomach & breasts but once I slipped on a t-shirt you couldn't tell.

Over the course of the infection, I manfully gargle hot salt water & touch the sores with my tongue tens of thousands of times a day.

When I arrive home after a trip, I usually wind up in a doctor's office, showing her a weepy rash: *Look what I found in my armpit!*

I get hives from budgies, cats, chinchillas, dogs, ferrets, gerbils, hamsters, mice & rats.

One time, I found a tick between my breasts. I marched to the door & threw it like a punch into the lilacs.

I deeply appreciated the doctor's shocked inspiration when I carefully took off my shirt.

Fly away.   *Fly away.*   Fly away, home.

How to Pack Without Overpacking

Fill three bags full of wool … or at least your carry-on. Knit what you need en-route. Only visit long-haired friends. Take your relationship 'to the next level' while in town & wrap them around you like an unwashed mohair blanket. Pack a lot of the same coloured clothes. Try not to think about the fact that your wrinkled all-beige ensembles make you look like you're on a heavy dose. Bring nothing. Be the liquid girl at the bar sobbing because her luggage was lost. Steal an item of clothing from every boy you pick up. (Urban cowboy hats don't count.) Sacrifice t-shirts like they're second sons: loved, wanted, but ultimately superfluous to the grand scheme. Hesitate but wield the knife expertly. Only buy clothes with secret pockets, zippered compartments & space-age fabrics. All trip long, spend evenings hunched over the sink, your mornings relishing the still-damp pong. Bring it all. When you set your bags down on the scale at the airport, speak to the steward in the same wheedling tone you'd use on a tetch-y horse. (Their noses are velvet, you know…) Be prepared to pay for your extra luggage as well as your impertinence. Subscribe to a 'packing philosophy.' Practice until you can fold a mound of person-shaped items into small perfect boxes. When you find yourself vacuuming the air out of your luggage, know you've arrived.

How to Write a Poem

Write about what terrifies you but, um, wait until mum or dad is dead to do it. For the family's sake…

Take all the punctuation out of your poem

Your lover should be your first reader & your subject, but know this: having good sex is hard. Writing good sex is harder. Believing someone who just had their head between your legs—even if they're a hardcore critic—impossible.

No one needs your next poem.
(Everyone needs your next goddamn poem.)

If writing rhyming poetry about God from jail, realize you've hit the trifecta. Celebrate by centering everything on the hard drive that's not porn.

capital letters are for suckers. seersuckers. sapsuckers.

Also, use the page. Engage the ear. Allude to classical texts, sneak in a few impeccable pop culture references. Break the line. Break a leg.

Have a firm grasp of grammar & syntax but also have something on the side with the fragment. Form should follow content but, hopefully, not breathing heavily.

Put the punctuation back in.

Don't write poems about writing poems.

4.

How to Soften Facial Scars

The veil over her face
a spider's web. She catches curious
eyes & wraps them for later consumption.
Her mouth hangs open

behind her veil as when she swam
in the pond at her grandfather's farm;
once she caught
a minnow, a silvery

tongue probing her teeth.
She swallowed.
The skin on her face wrapping
paper torn from a gift, smoothed out

& re-used. Her face a tissue-paper pattern
laid out on the table, cut
& pinned
but never made up.

Her mother's sewing scissors
gleamed in bolts of afternoon sunlight.
The muscles & fat & veins
over her skull—her real clothes—

impeccably tailored.
Muffled by linen & cambric & lace
her body language is rolled up
in a silk carpet & carried

out of the conversation.
But her eyes are outrageous, embroidered
with gold thread, her mother's careful stitches
showing. The bomb

was dirty, full of cutlery & iron
nails & bits of sheet metal.
It caught her like an unexpected
embrace. The nurses wept

as they unwound
the field dressings. The surgeon only
threaded his needle with gut
and got to work,

fingers tracing
every basted line. She doesn't sew,
hoards shed buttons
in a drawer where other women

would keep baby teeth or brittle
love letters. Her face an abused envelope,
herself a scented page
you will never put down.

Summer Weight

His eyes wreathed with bandages. My eyes filmed
with lines from the letter I'm writing him,
knowing someone will have to read it to him,
struggling with my idiosyncratic *eeeeeees*. When I am older,
I'll have to learn other languages. I'm told his eyes are light
sensitive. My clothes are dark mourning, summer weight.
My grandmother died last year & everything was bought
slightly big so I'd get more wear out of them. I don't sleep. I imagine
that under his bandages, the skin around his eyes
is as soft as breath. It takes an afternoon to persuade myself
to look away from his window. No one
told me to wear mourning, but no one has told me to take it off,
either. My hands are ink-stained. I want to bring him
a red squirrel's tail, the groundskeeper's boy taking aim
all afternoon. A cut-crystal wine glass, empty. A flight feather
from the goose we found, all ribcage & long bones, down
by the pond. I don't remember pushing him out
of the tree. But they say I did. When I am older I'll have to hide
my hair. The bandages wound around his blonde head: changed
every day, yellowing slowly. A book left in the sun,
pages curling. I have finished my letter.

How to Tell if Someone is Dead

You will be told she is dead, given some cursory explanation. Heart stoppage. Her comfortable old car t-boned on a dirt road. Her body sprawled in the imagination, undone. You will never see her again, but you will be Facebook™ friends forever.

*

The scab of feet & fur you find between boxes in the basement, come moving day.

A phone that falls between couch cushions & loses its charge.

A flashlight from the drawer, chalky with battery acid.

White-white fish bellies, bobbing at the surface.

Her stiffening body.

*

Her reluctant bellyaching is in no way absorbed by the beige walls of the waiting room. Immediate but pointless surgery, her abdomen a tank full of bleached coral & deep-sea creatures. Her shrunken, sheeted death, tubes everywhere. And you holding her hand, tight & useless …

*

Cough.

Her powdery compact mirror.

A poke to the ribs: poke Poke POKE. *C'mon!*

An onion, seeping on the cutting board.

A vicious pinch. Her soft belly.

*

She sleeps in. You leave her undisturbed through the morning, thinking, *She needs her sleep.* You try to make as little sound as possible at first, but then get bolder, your kettle whistling cheerfully mid-afternoon. But still, it is her right to sleep as long as she likes. And then you remember you need something in her room.

Song Of

Your armpit is a red squirrel torn
open on the road.

Your forearms are as cars left
at the curb, mid-summer: covered in aphid shit.
Which is to say you're mottled. But your shoulder
is a high-beam. A bare gleam.

Your ass is two feral cats
in the auto bin.

But without you, the streetlights won't
come on. I'm a sedan rattling down
the alley

& never coming home.

Apparent Magnitude: the Finlay 15P

> "William Henry Finlay (b. 17 June 1849 in Liverpool; d. 7 December 1924 in Cape Town, South Africa) was a South African astronomer. He was First Assistant at the Cape Observatory from 1873 to 1898. He discovered the periodic Comet 15P/Finlay. Earlier, he was one of the first to spot the 'Great Comet of 1882'."
> —"William Henry Finlay," *Wikipedia*

Mr. Finlay, you're a man of science…

And I realized she'd been leaning on the deck rail
beside me for some time. The voyage home
begun when my cousin's letter arrived,
    blue ink smeared.

…what, precisely, is the horizon?

I cleared my throat. Looked down
into her dark eyes. It is a moveable circle, I said,
reluctant. *Always as far away*
    as we can see.

She glanced at Cape Town's harbour, gleaming
in the flat sun behind us, feathers in the brim
of her hat moving in the breeze
    of our passage, sea-birds
        screaming overhead.

She opened her mouth again.

Practically everyone sees a different horizon,
I said quickly. And tipped my hat. Her eyes
on my back as I walked away.

The naked eye is my enemy.

*

My brother died after falling from the big tree in the yard, his arms outstretched, his back broken. After the doctor left, Mother made me release the animals in his backyard menagerie, bandaged animals limping into the woods. When I came in, his bulky sailor suit, folded up on the foot of my bed. I buried its rough blue at the back of my wardrobe while she accepted condolences from the neighbours. She cried into Father's neck afterwards, cried as a baby does, instantly & with notes of true pain. From the top of the stairs, from a great distance, I could see.

*

My brother staring out his open window, his brow furrowed as he contemplated the garden, his blue serge elbows on the sill. He had been confined to his room for an hour so I sat under the apple tree & waited. Mother had been doing calculations of her own from the kitchen & now sailed out of the house with the tray she used when we were sick held high.

When she reached the tree's shadowy skirts, she set the tray on the ground. Plates and napkins, cheese, cookies. *I've a trick for you,* she said. And reached up to palm two apples.

Sitting next to me on the ground, she took a paring knife from her right apron pocket & split the apples, showing me their five-pointed star. She handed me half, then, after a few bites, fished a pip from her mouth. She took a threaded needle from her left pocket and pierced the spit-shined seed. Handing me the needle, she gestured towards the gnawed cores, the pips on the plate. As I pushed its tip through a seed's dark heart, my focus both narrowing & widening, my brother called out, *Is it time yet, Mum?* Her bowls/his make-shift aquariums, soaking in the sink. Half-grown frogs & the shimmer of small fry returned to the pond. The sun moving across the lawn. And me, full of her & him. Full of stars & dark seeds, years of apples swallowed without thought, without consideration. *Is it time?*

*

They must have known, somehow, that I was going to move as far away as possible when I was grown.

I was middle-aged when I sighted my comet. Thirteen years polishing the hard wooden stool under the telescope.

*

Father's funeral.

After the soft parade is gone,
the barn swallow scissors
by the window in full sun: its swift shadow,
its forked tail on the wall
above my bed.

Close my eyes & I'm ten, hiding
under the hedgerow & its galaxy of dark
berries. How the birds spread its seeds
everywhere they flew
without knowing it.

Close my eyes. 1882. That tail. Anti-tail.
Its shattered nucleus after the transit: all of it visible
everywhere. Great comet. *Pah.*
Probably a piece of a piece of a comet.
Hundreds of years again before the two fragments
I documented would appear again
in the morning sky.

*

Mother kept me home from school, coming into my room at all hours & touching my cheek or my leg, her eyes slightly out of focus. Father took me out to his workshop in the evenings & powdered me with sawdust. We presented her with an ever-so-slightly askew table & the blackened half-moon on my thumbnail.

*

I spy on the nesting pair of barn swallows
from my old bedroom, twitching orange drapes
aside so I can see the male's apricot belly,
his split tail jutting
from the side of the mud-ball nest.

All are strong elegant fliers,
says the field guide on the bookshelf
next to the window, relevant pages marked
with scraps of paper.

Measure the birds' back-and-forth orbit
from the big tree to their nest in the rafters.
Note the mechanical drone
of insects
among my mother's tea roses,
some of the plants predating me.

It comes to me. The male's blue head
the same colour
as my brother's sailor suit.

*

I was back at school by the time the eclipse dimmed the sun. Father and I made a mask through which I could spy on the heavens. I thought everything was set, until one evening I heard her. *But his eyes, Lawrence. What if he damages his eyes, peering at the eclipse?* The day of the eclipse, I had permission to stay home, but she made me wear the sailor suit. Very early, she called me into the kitchen & dressed me as if I were a doll, my chest all goose pimples as her fingers worked. She sat back & looked at me. Then she took a ladle & went to the stove. Scooping up cooled ashes, she dipped her fingers & rubbed it into the sleepy skin around my eyes: split logs, kitchen scraps & newspaper twists. Long hours tending the fire. The puff of her warm breath on my cheeks as she leaned close. *There*, she said, with some gravity. And started building up the fire again as I burst through the back door.

*

Mr. Finlay, would you care to dance?

Her voice somehow full of certainty
that I would refuse her, preferring the hot breeze
over Cape Town, the night, to pinked cheeks & candlepower,
    the precise chill of the evening's entertainments.

I turned towards her, surrendering
my view. Her dark eyes
less sure than her voice.

*I'm afraid I never learned how to dance,
Miss McGrath.* I had seen

her at the lectures in town,
    writing in a little notebook, raising a gloved hand
        to ask questions,

        her set in a cluster
    of women, laughing, jewels at her throat
full of light. I believe her parents were missionaries.

I believe in nothing
except what Gill, Royal Astronomer,
calls "a long course of accurate work."

    *

Once safely inside the workshop, I stole father's second-best pipe, already packed full of tobacco. I sniffled but managed to light it, drawing carefully. Coughing, of course. Shooting stars across my field of vision. My true revenge came that afternoon. When the eclipse's slow burn was for my eyes only.

    *

My comet comes back every seven years. She's reliable.

They missed her the year after I retired.

(My father died alone.)

How to Survive a Plane Crash

> "Sept. 17, 1908. During a demonstration flight, a U.S. Army flyer flown by Orville Wright nose-dived into the ground from a height of approximately 75 feet, killing Lt. Thomas E. Selfridge who was a passenger. This was the first recorded airplane fatality in history."
> —planecrashinformation.blogspot.com.

A box kite with a motor, we say now, able to measure
every inch of its hundred-foot fall.
But we also know the soldiers on horseback
reached it first, the beasts rearing at smoke, blood and flapping
canvas, parading their best instincts. The last thing
the passenger heard, as the plane was lifted off
him? A screaming
horse.

A soldier, tumbled to the ground, his mare galloping
down the runway, is glad of the rebellion: *This is not safe,*
she is saying, air beneath her hooves but never
fully flying.

At ground level, the crash site is a heap of linen pulled
from the line and trampled. The crash site is a treed kite, yanked
down. The crash site is the whites of eyes, the weight
of eyes tracing the plane's trajectory, plotting
its descent.

The soldier sees the pilot turn his head, mutter *Please take care
of my leg*, but the crash site is crowded: stuttering cars abandoned,
keys in the ignition. Rows and rows of onlookers,
each braced against the ribs and shoulders

of another, a phalanx that attempted the plane's weak spots
even before it left the ground.

(Each of them a screw loose,
a rotor turning wrong.)

So the soldier stays put. And the chalky dust rises, a cloud
that could have kept the plane air-borne
but all the pilot got
in the air
was bared throats
and staccato puffs: *oh! Oh!*

OH!

The chalk blinked from the eyes
of stretcher-bearers. The chalk gilding the insignia
of the other soldiers, their linked hands keeping the crowd
back from the powdered hair and twisted
limbs of the pilot, the bloody sigh
of the passenger.

The soldier lies on the ground, watching a bird
on the roof of the mechanic's shed a little ways off.
It is small. Drab. He admires how it looks down
from its great height and refrains from singing.

In the hospital, the pilot cleared his throat
and asked for his mechanic. *I'd like to have his view
on just what happened to cause our spill*, he says, jovial,
but almost unable to meet the eyes of the reporters.

In the hospital, the pilot had a box of wreckage
brought to him, its weight on his shattered
leg, his battered pelvis.

Grimy, taped shut, the box could be a model, a kit
sent to amuse him in his convalescence. It could be a parcel
from an aunt abroad, his stomach seized
with anticipation and dread: *What is it?*

Opened, the box shows chalk coating everything still,
blades of grass and what could be grease
and what could be gore
on parts pulled
from the crash site.

(One man clasped the other as they plunged.
One man cried a little but the onrush took the tears
so in the end, each appeared dry
and remorseless.)

NOTES

The transcribed bird calls interspersed throughout the collection come from The Cornell Lab of Ornithology's *All About Birds* website: www.allaboutbirds.org.

Bicker
"It is strangely quiet here today without the familiar screech of the Merlins."—Carolyn Curtis, Merlins thread, Manitobabirds message board.

"We (the wildlife branch) receive numerous calls from Manitoba & Wpg residents each year wondering how they can get rid of or scare off their Merlins. Like you they object to their noisiness & the fact they scare off many of the nice birds from their neighborhood. No doubt you are glad to get some peace and quiet back in the neighbourhood. The question is, do you look forward to their return next year?"—Ken De Smet, Manitoba Conservation and Water Stewardship. Ibid.

Lures
For Anita Daher. For loaning us her riverhouse, those times we needed it.

Heart Attack
For Michael Van Rooy, 1968-2011.

Picked Out
"Fruit Share connects fruit owners with surplus fruit with volunteer fruit pickers. These volunteers pick the fruit and share it between the fruit owners, the volunteers and community groups." — "How Does it Work," Fruit Share Manitoba.

Little White Lie
"The beluga is the only whale with a flexible neck. (Their vertebrae remain unfused.) Sometimes, curious whales will turn and look up at

you as they pass near your boat."—"Beluga Whales in the Churchill River," churchillscience.ca.

Mother Goose
"Canada Geese prefer nest sites near water with a good view of the surrounding area. Geese may sometimes nest in less than ideal habitats such as landscaped areas in parking lots, on planters, balconies or rooftops."—"Best Practices for Destroying Eggs or Preventing Hatching," Environment Canada.

Little Pig
"A barn housing pregnant sows is called a gestation barn. A pregnant sow delivers her piglets in a farrowing room, which has supplemental heat and an appropriate floor surface for the sow and piglet."—"How Pigs Are Raised," Manitoba Pork Council.

Herd Instinct
"Your adventure begins as your guide leads you through the aspen forest onto the open prairie, where your heart leaps as you catch your first up-close view of 30 grunting, munching herbivores—the bison, North America's largest land animal." —"A Prairie Legacy: The Bison and its People," Fort Whyte Alive.

Canis soupus
"Coyotes are a common wildlife species throughout North America. They have adapted well to man's artificial landscape and they seem equally comfortable living in city suburbs as they do out on the prairie. Coyotes are most common in the agricultural areas of Manitoba, but now range into the boreal forest and as far North as Flin Flon and Thompson. The total number of coyotes is virtually impossible to estimate but they are considered abundant. Coyotes are now seen more frequently in urban and suburban centres of Manitoba."—"Coyotes: Living with Wildlife in Manitoba," Manitoba Conservation and Water Stewardship.

The title of this poem refers to the coyote's ability to breed with dogs and wolves, creating a hearty 'soup' of genetic material.

How to Tell if Someone is Dead
This poem had its beginning in the sudden/inexplicable deaths of Robert Kroetsch and Michael Van Rooy in 2011. Bah!

Apparent Magnitude
This poem is for Darryl Joel Berger, who hooked me with a painting of an evil-looking little boy in a sailor suit with shadows under his eyes & a pipe in his mouth on an encyclopedia page that included the orbit of the Finlay comet.

ACKNOWLEDGEMENTS

Poems in *Stowaways* appeared in the following magazines and websites: *Carousel Magazine, Contemporary Verse 2, Earthlines, Room Magazine,* and Leaf Press' *Monday's Poem.*

Sections of this manuscript also appeared as chapbooks from Saskatoon's JackPine Press and Vernon's Kalamalka Press (after my submission won the inaugural John Lent Poetry-Prose Award in 2012).

"Blown" and "How to Survive a Plane Crash" were finalists for *Arc Magazine*'s Poem of the Year contest, in 2012 and 2009 respectively. "Primipara" will appear in the essay of the same name in *The M Word: Conversations about Motherhood*, edited by Kerry Clare and published by Goose Lane Editions in spring 2014.

I'm a sucker for art/writing cross-pollination, so I'm grateful to Kirsten at *Papirmass: Art in the Mail* and Janine at *Uppercase Magazine* for including my work between their covers.

Thanks to Dawn Kresan at Palimpsest, for asking after these poems, for forcing them to coalesce into a manuscript. To Jim Johnstone, for helping me turn the manuscript into a book. And to kevin eckhoff mcpherson and Julie Bruck for the magnificent blurbs.

This book was created with the generous support of the City of Winnipeg through the Winnipeg Arts Council. Laura Lamont (and her mum) & Anita Daher also deserve mention for loaning me their respective cabins-in-the-woods.

Acknowledgement is due to the members of the Plastered Hams—Alison Calder, Kerry Ryan & Jennifer Still—for their help in thinking and feeling my way through the poems. Also for the baking, though mine is always store-bought…

Thanks too to Amy Karlinsky and the participants in the Readings & Creative Writing for Artist Mothers class at Mentoring Artists for Women's Art (MAWA) in fall 2011, for helping me to get to my first 'weremummy' poem.

Also essential throughout these years of writing—and discarding writing—were Yvonne Blomer, GMB Chomichuk, Marita Dachsel, David Jon Fuller, Tracy Hamon, kevin eckhoff mcpherson, Brenda Schmidt, Bren Simmers, Anna Swanson, and John Toone.

Special thanks to Darryl Joel Berger, writer/visual artist/graphic designer, who is worse than me in all ways AND whose images were the inspiration for many of the poems.

To all of you, I say: more writing/drawing/comics! MORE!

Finally, thanks to Mike and Anna. For most everything else, including leaving the house so I could write these (goddamn) acknowledgements.

AUTHOR BIOGRAPHY

Ariel Gordon is a Winnipeg writer. Her first book of poetry, *Hump*, won the 2011 Aqua Books Lansdowne Prize for Poetry. Most recently, her chapbook *How to Make a Collage* won Kalamalka Press' inaugural John Lent Poetry-Prose Award. When not being bookish, Ariel likes tromping through the woods and taking macro photographs of mushrooms.